TURKEYS AND EAGLES

TURKEYS AND EAGLES

by Peter Lord

Christian Books Publishing House
Auburn, Maine

DEDICATION

To a true eagle whose soaring in all of life's situations has been an inspiration and challenge to me to be who I am in Christ, my friend Jack Taylor.

ACKNOWLEDGEMENT

This book is the result of a single message taken from a cassette and made ready for publication by three people to whom I owe a deep debt of gratitude. Without them the book would never have been written. Thank you Marian Clark, Rick Cain, and Gene Edwards.

PREFACE

We are all in danger of falling into the same trap that Adam and Eve fell into.

They were tempted to become something they already were.

The devil said, "If you eat . . . you will be like God."

They were *already* like God. Made in the image and in His likeness. They could not have been any more like God without being God. God made them as much like Him as He could.

If the evil one can keep us from knowing who and what we are in Christ Jesus — new creations, saints, the people and children of God — then he can tempt us to act, by making us want what we think we do not have.

The Christian does not do in order to become. He does because He is what God has made him in Christ Jesus.

Peter Lord

INTRODUCTION

"It's hard to soar with the eagles when you live with turkeys."

That is a popular statement of our day. When I first heard it I asked myself, "Why are eagles keeping company with turkeys in the first place?" I would like to share a story with you that the Lord has given to me that was inspired chiefly by that statement — "turkeys and eagles."

But before you read the story, may I first ask you to take a short test. There are thirteen questions in all, the first nine are true-false. Do not study each question. Answer them with your heart's first impression. After completing the test, set it aside until you have finished reading the story, then let us look at the questions again.

Ready?

TEST

T F 1. A good description of a Christian is a sinner saved by grace.

T F 2. You can sin and not know it.

T F 3. It is normal for Christians to sin every day.

T F 4. A bad thought is a sin.

T F 5. It is easier for a Christian to sin than to do right.

T F 6. The closer we get to Christ, the less we will be tempted.

T F 7. We get closer to Christ through actions of righteousness.

T F 8. Sainthood is attained by only a few Christians.

T F 9. To be tempted is a sign of our sinfulness.

10. How many sins have you committed today? (You may have to approximate.)

11. How many acts of righteousness have you committed today?

12. How righteous is Jesus Christ on a scale of one to a hundred?

13. How righteous are you on a scale of one to a hundred?

And now that you have taken this little test, read the story which follows. At the close of the book we will look at the answers to this test to see if you have been turkey-sized.

PART I

1

Nata had been worried about her newly hatched eaglet from the moment he emerged from his shell. This was her very first eaglet, and she had not anticipated so small and fragile a creature. Why, he could not even lift his head. Furthermore, she had repeatedly offered food to him, yet he had not taken note of her offer.

Lovingly she gazed at that one other egg which had so far refused to hatch. This egg was light brown in color with splotches of black. This exquisite egg lay nestled next to the new eaglet, who lay among the leaves and grass lacing the nest. Now eagles call their nest an aerie, and this one consisted of interwoven sticks and brush covered on the outside with gray-green moss so that it might blend with the gray rock of the cliff on which it rested.

"Papa is on his way," Nata thought as she gazed toward the descending sun.

At that very moment Ramon was gliding effortlessly above a grassy clearing in the wood. His wings, spreading out more than six feet in width, held the awe-inspiring bird aloft with ease as he looked for food. Ramon had stout legs and strong feet, with talons as sharp as steel. His sturdy beak was nearly as long as his head. One flap of his mighty wings held him soaring aloft for as long as an hour while his keen eyes looked for food. His feathers were blackish-brown with a golden wash on the back of the neck. There was a bob of white at the base of his tail and at the tips of his wings.

Suddenly, his superb eyesight caught a movement about 400 yards to his right, a movement so slight that it would not have been noticeable to the human eye. Ramon's prey was a small rabbit. He glided into a turn and flew level for an instant. Then suddenly, swooping down with lightning speed, Ramon snagged his unsuspecting prey without a sound.

Ramon lifted proudly into the sky, knowing once again he was a good provider for Nata and the precious eaglets in his aerie.

"Here comes dinner," Nata said softly as she watched the distant silhouette of Ramon come into view.

"Why do you continue to worry, Nata?" asked Ramon, trying not to show his impatience as he dropped the broken rabbit at Nata's feet. Ramon was clearly irritated at the look of anxiety on her face. Before she could answer, he spoke again. "The little one is getting stronger. See, he is moving about more. Do not worry about him. Soon, after the other egg hatches and both of them are strong enough to move about, I will throw a great party for our friends to celebrate the arrival of our new eaglets!"

Nata was trying hard to share her husband's excitement. True, they were her first eaglets, but Ramon was convinced they would both prove to be perfectly healthy. Nata made a conscious decision to not worry about her little brood anymore.

Sure enough, the second eaglet hatched just two days after the first. Nata was elated to discover that she now had a boy eaglet and a girl eaglet. The boy she named Hagen, for he was small and fragile. The girl eaglet, on the other hand, was not small at all, nor was she frail. "She shall fly higher than any eagle has ever flown before," Nata whispered to herself. "I will call her Selin."

As the next few days passed, she began to get excited about the upcoming party. She was convinced that all the other eagles would think her eaglets were the most beautiful they had ever seen.

On the day of the party, the sky was filled with eagles soaring in from far distant places. Nata could not remember a time when she had seen so many eagles in one place. She and her two eaglets were greeted with overwhelming enthusiasm. Giving birth to two such precious creatures had been, of course, a wonderful occasion for her, but now she could clearly see that her two little ones were just as great a cause for celebration for the eagle community as they were for her. Occasions of this kind were rare among eagles, for their population had been steadily declining in recent years. This day, therefore, was one of great joy, hope and festivity. And, as is so often true of such grand celebrations, everyone was taking advantage of it.

The rejoicing went on for the entire day. The sun was beginning to set when the eagles began to say goodbye. After the last eagle had lifted high into the sky, disappearing in the sun, Ramon turned proudly toward Nata. She had lived with Ramon long enough to recognize the look upon his face. It was a look of ambition, a thing which often came upon Ramon.

"Nata, dear, wasn't this the most wonderful day of your life!? Our friends had nothing but praise for our beautiful eaglets. What we have done together is indeed a wonderful thing to behold. We have brought new eagles into this world! What is there in all the earth or sky that could be greater?

"This is what we were created for!" Ramon exclaimed as his eyes burned with excitement.

Nata had seen Ramon enthusiatic about many things in past seasons, but she realized this last statement was apparently a great, new revelation to him; she could not remember him ever becoming quite this elated.

"We must move, Nata, and build another aerie. We are going to do it again!" Ramon cried, his voice filled with obvious glee. "To renew this land, to replenish the skies with the great eagles, that is our life!"

Nata was not as confident about Ramon's ideas as he was, but she knew that he always meant well, and she trusted him. They decided to begin their new work immediately.

I am quite sure you will find it hard to believe when I tell you that Ramon and Nata immediately set off to build a new aerie, and in so doing, totally abandoned their two young eaglets. Of course, they surely intended to return to check on the well-being of their little ones, but building an aerie requires a tremendous amount of work. And, as so often happens in situations like this, Ramon and Nata entirely forgot about their little eaglets in their dedication to having yet another brood of eaglets. (It is rumored that these were Baptist eagles!)

The next morning Hagen awoke cold and hungry. So too did his sister, Selin. They waited patiently all day for Mama and Papa to return. By afternoon, though, they knew they would have to act soon to survive if Mama and Papa did not return immediately.

As Hagen searched the sky, he asked Selin anxiously, "Do you have any suggestions?"

Selin peeked over the side of the aerie, only to discover that it had been built on a ledge of a rock some 300 feet above the ground. Remember, Hagen and Selin were only a few weeks old and knew nothing about flying. "This is now our third day alone and without food," Selin replied weakly. "We must surely get down and find something to eat."

Hagen, hoping that his sister *knew* how they would "get down," asked, "And how shall we accomplish this feat?"

"We have to jump," she said calmly.

Hagen quickly moved away from the edge of the nest.

"Jump!?!" he screeched, incredulous. "If we do, we will surely die. You cannot be serious!"

8

Selin did not like the idea any more than her brother did, but what else could they do? "We are going to die anyway," she replied.

"All right," said Hagen, "but let us wait a little longer. If Mama isn't back *very* soon, then we will . . . we will . . . decide what to do."

The rest of the afternoon was spent agonizing over a decision that contained few choices. It was obvious to both that they really had no alternative but to chance a death-defying jump.

"If we stay here, we *are* going to die," Selin said with finality.

"And if we jump, we will *probably* die," came Hagen's meek reply.

"You and I really cannot do *anything* until we learn to fly," Hagen said in a moment of revelation. Struck by the truth of his words, he leaned back in dejection.

But at last the two eaglets agreed that they were not only hungry and cold, but also near death. So they moved to the side of their aerie, closed their eyes, held their breath and jumped.

Two blood-curdling screeches followed, along with the frantic flapping of wings. Then silence.

2

Hagen was certain he was dead, but he opened his eyes just to be sure. After a few moments of checking out his extremities he discovered to his amazement that he was not only alive but whole. Cautiously, Hagen rose to his feet. A few feet away Selin was also struggling to rise.

Selin looked up to see if she could find the aerie they had just jumped from, but it was impossible, for the aerie was hidden by the ledge. Neither of our two little eaglets could believe they had fallen from such heights and lived. Of course, part of the reason for their survival was all that flapping, and part of it was that they had fallen in a soft, grassy area.

It took only a moment for both Hagen and Selin to remember why they had risked their lives in such a venture; their weak legs and trembling bodies told them they were on the verge of starvation.

"Where are we?" Selin asked softly.

"At the edge of a great wooded forest, it seems," Hagen replied, as he studied the dark and mysterious area that lay to his left.

"Should we look for food in there?" Selin asked in a whisper.

"I do not think we belong in there," Hagen sensed. "We need to stay out in the open air where we can feel the wind."

"How do you know that?" Selin asked curiously. She felt the same way, but she did not know why. Neither Mama nor Papa had taught them anything about survival. In fact, their parents had not taught them *anything, not even that they were eagles.*

Hagen made no reply to Selin's question. He was not sure why he did not want to go into the wood. It just did not seem right to him.

Just ahead of them could be seen an open meadow that stretched before them for what seemed like forever. At least it was a lot bigger than a nest! Beyond the meadow the two eaglets could see an immense mountain range. "Aren't they . . . absolutely beautiful," Hagen said as he stared at the mountains, while at the same time wondering why he was so drawn to them.

You see, there is something deep within an eagle that is just naturally drawn to great heights; that is just the way it is with eagles. Even with eagles who do not know they are eagles. The wide open meadow which lay before Hagen and Selin was inviting, but those great mountains seemed literally to cry out to them.

This moment of revery was suddenly interrupted by a noise coming from within the nearby wood. Instinctively the two young eaglets lunged toward one another.

"It is coming from the wood," Selin said breathlessly.

"And it is getting closer," Hagen added.

From out of the edge of the wood slowly emerged some strange looking birds.

"One of us?" Hagen whispered.

"I . . . I don't know," Selin replied.

What the two young eaglets were staring at was a flock of earth-bound turkeys out on a leisurely hunt for food.

Now it is not a good idea to startle turkeys. They stampede very easily. And that is almost what happened. Upon seeing Hagen and Selin the turkeys began to cackle furiously and run around in circles, creating a totally meaningless commotion. As a result, everyone ended up frightened out of their wits. When the dust had cleared, Hagen watched spellbound as two beady little eyes peered down at him.

"Hello," Hagen said to the two eyes, the strange face and the long, skinny neck. "We are very sorry we scared you. We heard you in the wood. You see, we are trying to find food, and we fell out of that nest, and we are hungry, and we do not know where we are, and . . ."

"Don't you fear, little fella," gobbled out the huge old turkey who had been eyeing Hagen.

"One of us?" Hagen asked himself silently.

Hagen and Selin studied their new acquaintance with great curiosity. This strange bird stood taller than any bird they had ever seen. His body was broad and fat, his legs long and skinny. He had something that looked like a beard which was so long it almost dragged on the ground. This queer-looking creature had a bald head with a snood protruding right out of the middle of his forehead. Even so, this odd bird *was* strutting proudly. Maybe he was the same kind of bird they were, just one that was sort of funny looking.

"What with the way things are out here, one can't be too careful," bellowed the big turkey in his irritating but friendly voice. "Excuse the commotion, we always raise a fuss when something startles us. Now what was it you said

14

you two little turkeys were doing out here all alone?"

"Turkeys?" Hagen exclaimed in awe.

"We are looking for food," Selin replied softly.

"Looking for food, huh? You'll be food if you stay out here by yourself very long. Where is your Mama and Papa?"

"We do not know," Selin said sadly as she threw up her little wings in wonder.

Hagen thought for a moment about what the turkey had just said. "Be food?!" he shrieked. "What do you mean? Surely nothing could eat us."

The turkey laughed out loud. This time he turned to the other turkeys, motioning for them to come join him as he did. Soon they were all laughing as one, and in the process, making quite a clatter.

After a moment the great turkey turned again to Hagen, this time with a caring look upon his skinny old face. "We don't mean to make fun of you, but you obviously don't know what a forest is like. You must always be on the lookout. You see, we turkeys have many enemies, and *they* want nothing more than to eat us."

Hagen stood dumbfounded as he watched all the other turkeys nodding in agreement.

"You may join us, little ones, if you so desire. We would be delighted to have you among us. We will do our very best to take care of you and to raise you in the finest turkey tradition, to be wise, strong and proud turkeys," the big turkey said solemnly and with great finality. "My name is Brant. And what might be your names?" the great turkey asked in a most reassuring manner.

"My name is Hagen and this is my sister Selin," Hagen said very formally, trying to imitate the turkey's sober demeanor to match this obviously important occasion. But inside, Hagen was beginning to feel very dependent on his new friend.

Brant now turned to introduce Hagen and Selin to the other turkeys. Everyone was extremely courteous and friendly to Hagen and Selin, and they felt welcomed. These formalities concluded, Brant, realizing that his two little friends were in desperate need of sustenance, suggested that the entire party now continue their search for food.

So it was that just a few minutes later the little eaglets got their first taste of turkey food. It was something the turkeys called "acorns." The two were so starved that the acorns tasted better than anything they had ever dreamed of. This food was so good, in fact, that they were quite certain they would enjoy it forever. At least, they were sure they would live. And they owed it all to their new-found *fellow* turkeys!

Strange, is it not, that one can feel so welcomed and so received, yet not quite feel at home. And as the days passed, this strange feeling grew. Neither Hagen or Selin could put their beak on it, but each knew something was amiss, despite the fact that they were loved and accepted.

The place they came to realize the greatest difference was in those acorns and in the hunting of them. Hagen often asked himself, "This is not how Papa looked for food. . . . Well, was it?"

Those acorns! Yes, it is true that at first the acorns tasted delicious. But lately those things had grown more foul-tasting with every peck.

The other thing that bothered Hagen was appearance. He spent a good part of his free moments looking at the other little turkey-ettes (they called themselves turkey chicks). Hagen thought that perhaps his sister Selin looked a bit like those other little turkeys, and this thought really bothered him — for it meant he might also look like them!

Soon Brant began to sense the uneasiness of the two new turkeys. He felt a great deal of compassion for them. He had often dealt with outsiders, and was familiar with their needs. He knew exactly how to meet those needs, and was quite sure they would settle in just as soon as they felt completely one with their new group. Furthermore, he was right.

You see, when an eagle cannot find his true home (no matter how hard he searches) he will eventually go anywhere he feels welcome. An eagle longs for love and acceptance, and he will respond to acceptance even if it is coming from turkeys. Never mind that these are not really the ones he would first choose to run around with. Acceptance is acceptance, no matter where you have to go to get it.

One day, Brant motioned to Hagen, Selin, and two other turkeys to come over to him.

"Hagen and Selin," Brant said. "Please hear me. We would like both of you to know how much it means to us that you have come to be with us. It is a privilege for us to have you." The two turkeys striding nearby nodded their full agreement.

"I would be honored to help you hunt, Selin," one of the turkeys volunteered.

"And I could be your partner, Hagen, if you'd like," the other said, appearing very excited about the idea.

Hagen and Selin were taken by surprise at such an obvious and sincere show of affection. You see, they had almost begun to believe that they were not turkeys and did not fit in here at all. But they could not help but respond to this warm acceptance which was being so freely extended to them.

Feeling better about themselves and trying to forget the differences which they seemed to feel between themselves and their new family, Hagen and Selin vowed anew to work at their relationship with their fellow turkeys. Sure enough, a few minutes later they had trotted off through the forest with their new hunting partners, looking for that horrible-tasting food which all turkeys eat.

One thing that still bothered Hagen, though, was the habit all the turkeys had of looking down in order to hunt for food. Hagen felt he should be eyeing his food first from a far distance and then, somehow, swooping down on it. He did not understand his feeling, but then he did not understand this groveling for food either.

"Obviously," he thought, "I must not be a good student of food gathering. I will watch more carefully how it is done."

Just then he heard Brant call out that he had found food. The turkeys all converged under a giant oak tree where Brant was proudly standing. "Help yourself!" he beamed. "Look at them. Acorns! Everywhere!"

"Ugh," Hagen thought. "I feel sick. I thought for sure he had found something new and good and refreshing to eat. But this is the same old stuff!"

Hagen and Selin stood watching in disbelief at the excitement with which all the other turkeys welcomed those 'tasty' acorns.

Of course, an acorn is a quite normal food for you, if you happen to be a turkey, but if you happen to be an eagle, well, eagles just should not have to eat acorns (unless the eagle happens to be starving; then he will eat even acorns to keep from dying.)

Not wanting to disappoint their new family, Hagen and Selin took a deep breath, waddled properly over to the oak tree and began cramming their craws with acorns.

The horrid things were incredibly dry and tasteless. The two eaglets-turned-turkeys soon felt so nauseous they dared not move. While standing there, Hagen had an almost uncontrollable urge to charge off into the sky just to get away from this whole horrid thing called turkeydom.

Instead, Hagen just stood there vowing over and over to himself that he *would be a good turkey* whatever the cost. Even if it meant eating acorns. This was very hard for Hagen to do. How hard? About as hard as if you were to vow, ever so courageously, to eat your daily newspaper for breakfast every morning!

That shows you just how far folks will go to be accepted by others, even if those others are of lower calling and purpose.

This is a fact well worth remembering: When it seems that you have nowhere to go, you will always end up where you are welcome. And when an "outsider" feels that he has been accepted "in," he will often try to imitate the actions of his new peers to *assume* his acceptance.

Of course, *you* realize something Hagen did not. This misconception of acceptance forces us to deny our most instinctive ways just to win acceptance. The others seem to sense this, too. So they make change a prerequisite of acceptance!

One of the greatest needs of turkeys and eagles — and others — is that, after one has filled his craw, he still needs something else: acceptance and security.

If eagles don't meet that basic need in other eagles, well, as you can see, a turkey will!

If you do not extend love to other eagles, chances are a turkey will find him, and love him.

That is one of the most common ways that eagles become turkeys.

3

Days turned to weeks and, little by little, Hagen and Selin finally began to learn the ways of being proper turkeys. Brant, in turn, took great pride in his new students. He had trained many pupils in his time, but there was something special about these two, especially Hagen, for he tried so very, very hard.

Of course, Brant did have to spend an unusual amount of time teaching Hagen to like acorns. Hagen, in turn, worked hard to develop a taste for the dreadful things. At times, he even believed he was beginning to enjoy them. But we must be honest in reporting that a rumor did make the rounds that maybe, just maybe, Hagen was only saying this to please Brant.

Besides acorns, Hagen and Selin also took lessons in liking scratching. They did fairly well, but looking down and bending down seemed terribly unnatural to both of them, not to mention the ache it caused in their muscles.

There was one thing which really dumbfounded Brant; he had to teach these two young turkeys to be afraid. He even had to teach them to hide from their enemies. This was puzzling, as all turkeys were just naturally afraid ... of almost everything. On the other hand, these two did not seem to fear anything. Not at first, anyway. But they were studying hard and gradually they seemed to be learning how to be afraid.

There were also strutting lessons, pecking lessons and voice lessons for Hagen and Selin. These two turkeys just could not seem to gobble at all. In fact, Brant had to spend the greater portion of their lesson time just working on gobbling. Beyond that, the screech these two turkeys let out on occasion was the most fearsome thing he had ever heard in all his life. It sent a chill through his spine all the way up to his snood. It was a screech that reverberated with some primordial cry of joy and freedom. Brant hoped dreadfully that they would soon forget how to make this awful noise.

Anyway, the two young eaglets worked diligently at being turkeys. Brant, in turn, insisted that their tutors stay with them day and night so that they might never forget, even for a moment, how to act like proper turkeys.

Hagen did learn. But as he did, with each passing day he also became more and more frustrated.

A question began to gnaw at him: "Why is it that I am the only turkey in the world having trouble being a turkey?" His conclusion was obvious. "I must be the worst, most vile turkey who ever lived!"

This is a very difficult problem, is it not? When you are a turkey, it is very simple and natural to act like a turkey. But when you are an eagle, it is extremely difficult to be a turkey. It seems that no matter how hard you try, you always feel like a failure.

Sad to say, Hagen and Selin had, at last, been turkey-ized, and still they felt like utter failures. I wonder if this has ever happened to anyone else??

4

One morning, as Hagen moved through the woods with the flock of his fellow turkeys, he noticed in the distance that there was a turkey hen sitting in some deep grass. In fact, it appeared as though she were hiding from all the rest of the turkeys. Inquisitive as he was, Hagen could not pass by so strange a sight, so he angled his way toward the turkey hen.

Rad, a respected and admired turkey who often acted as sort of a pastor to the flock, watched Hagen in his maneuvering. Remembering Hagen's struggle with his role as a turkey, Rad gobbled out, "Hagen, wait for me!"

Hagen stopped and spun around. This was the first time Rad had ever spoken to him.

Rad was a huge turkey, so by the time he reached Hagen, he was quite winded.

"I've been wanting to . . . spend some . . . (Rad bent forward to catch his breath) time . . . with you. Let's walk this way and talk for a while." Rad pointed to a direction which led away from the hen.

Hagen resisted a little at first but then turned, hesitantly, with Rad. Hagen then asked, "Why is that hen hiding in the grass?"

Rad chuckled and answered, "She is sitting on her nest. She is concealing it from our enemies!" Rad relaxed a little now, realizing that Hagen was only curious, and not trying to escape turkeydom.

Bewildered, Hagen asked, "She is sitting on her nest?"

"That's right. She's mothering her eggs. It won't be long now before we have some new little turkeys among us," Rad boasted gently.

"But what is her nest doing on the ground?" Hagen persisted.

"What do you mean?" Rad asked, in a voice that betrayed his confusion. "Where do you think the nest should be?"

"My sister and I were born *high* . . ." Hagen hesitated. Just saying that word was like a song in his heart. "We were born . . . above all this."

The memory of the aerie seemed so far away that for a moment he wondered if it were only a dream. Maybe, he thought, he *had* been born on the ground. Maybe he was just a very confused little turkey who needed to work a little harder at being a turkey.

That, of course, is exactly what Brant and the other turkeys had been telling him. At last, Hagen knew he must stop feeding those strange notions he felt so deep within him. He had to give up all else and act only as the turkey that he was.

Rad stared into Hagen's eyes. He was dark-colored; his beard touched the ground. It was Rad's size which most impressed Hagen. You see, among turkeys, the fatter you are, the more admiration you gain from your fellow turkeys. You are considered to be wiser and more in line with the ways of an ancient (and most highly revered) turkey named Sacretoes. Sacretoes was known to be the greatest and wisest turkey ever to live in all the history of turkeydom.

"My, how great must be Rad," Hagen thought. "When he stands in front of me his size blocks out the view of anything else."

"Hagen, my boy," Rad began softly, "I think it is time I tell you where you came from. I intended to wait until you were much older before talking with you, but after watching your struggles for several weeks now, I think it is time you know."

"What are you saying?" Hagen said with a shuffle, his heart sinking as he spoke.

Rad hesitated for a moment. "All of us turkeys have to learn to take our place in life. We all have our share of struggles along the way, but you, Hagen . . . you are in for an even harder time."

Hagen could no longer look up at Rad. For the first time in his life Hagen let his proud wings drop to the ground.

"You see," Rad said, compassionately, "you were actually hatched from a *buzzard egg.*" Rad paused to let this dreadful revelation sink in.

Hagen did not move.

"No doubt you've noticed your physical difference from the rest of us, Hagen. You and your sister were born poor, wretched buzzards." He paused again and waited to catch Hagen's eye. "Look at me," Rad spoke demandingly. "There is nothing we can do about your hooked beak and your short legs, nor that you were born a poor, miserable buzzard! But we can give you a new heart. The heart of a turkey!"

Hagen was not too surprised by Rad's words. He had known from the moment he met the turkeys that he did not really fit in. But his heart sank to the absolute bottom as the awful truth seeped into him. "I am a buzzard. Selin is a buzzard. Good-for-nothing, low-down, hopeless buzzards."

(Now, *everyone* knows that buzzards are the most disgusting of all birds. Surely, then, you can know how Hagen felt. How would you like to be told that you were a poor, lost, wretched buzzard?)

"What do I do?" Hagen asked pitifully.

"First you must realize — and accept — the fact that you are a poor, lost, wretched, miserable, worthless buzzard, saved by turkeys!

"Secondly, it is normal for you to struggle with your *buzzardliness* every day. This will go on all your life. And yes, it will be a terrible struggle. You must persevere. And you must deal with this terrible fact every day. You are a poor, miserable buzzard. This is just a natural and normal part of your life. Don't ever forget it. But, don't ever let it get you down. Don't let it overpower you. Fight it! Struggle! Resolve!"

"I do not want to be a buzzard. How do I become a better turkey?" Hagen cried.

"Hagen, you *are* a turkey now. You've been saved from *buzzardom*. But never forget your dark, bleak side. You can be acting like a buzzard and not even be aware of it. Always be on the watch for that side of you to rise up. Dedicate your life to fighting the buzzardliness in you. And when you fail — and you will fail often — then re-dedicate your life!"

Hagen's eyes began to blur. His legs bent. How

could he live with so terrible a truth, so wretched a state, so awful a weight?

Compassion filled the heart of Rad as he saw this awful revelation grasp the heart of poor Hagen. Rad spoke again, quietly and with great comfort. "Oh, Hagen, do not let these facts discourage you. You must keep standing and fighting. Be encouraged by this: You have all the rest of the turkeys in the world standing with you. Furthermore, we will teach you to know the ways of Sacretoes. And most of all, remember this: *Once a turkey, always a turkey!"*

5

Months had passed since that fateful day Hagen and Selin plunged from their aerie and fell to the ground and were adopted by a flock of turkeys. Hagen was still having an extremely difficult time living the turkey life. His sister, on the other hand, seemed to be settling into her role much more easily. Observing this, Hagen's sense of guilt and worthlessness grew even greater. In the meantime, Rad had suggested to Brant that the 'two odd ones' not spend too much time together, as that only served to feed their problems of dealing with the 'sacred traditions of turkey life.'

Sure enough, Hagen and Selin were separated and rarely saw one another after that. Selin, unlike

Hagen, did not ask as many questions as she once had. Furthermore, she had disciplined herself not to make a contorted face or gag when she ate acorns. And though she looked very weird doing it, she had even learned to walk, more or less, like the other turkeys. By poking her feathers out as far as she could and by stretching her neck as far as possible, she made a fair imitation of a turkey's walk.

Observing Selin's success had brought Hagen to a state of utter hopelessness. Dragging his way behind the brood of turkeys one afternoon, Hagen noticed in the far distance another flock of turkeys coming slowly toward them. Neither flock had yet noticed the other. Only Hagen's sharp eye had detected the presence of the other turkeys.

These turkeys, he noticed, were not searching the ground for food as did his flock. Rather, they were pecking and pulling on branches. These turkeys were eating berries from bushes!

Hagen was astonished. He could only remember two or three occasions when he had seen one of his fellow turkeys eating a berry, and then only because the berry had fallen to the ground. But this turkey flock was pulling berries directly from the bush! "What a novel idea!" Hagen thought.

Hagen quickly sought out Brant. "Brant, look, over there, more turkeys! And they are coming this way! And they are eating . . ."

"Where?" Brant shouted in alarm. He quickly gave a signal of danger to the other turkeys. "I don't see any other turkeys," Brant insisted nervously.

Hagen and Selin realized *none* of their fellow turkeys seemed to be able to see as far and as clearly as they could.

(How could this be? Is it not true that turkeys also have excellent eyesight? Yes, but it seems they have focused their vision so narrowly, for so long, that they now see only those things which they have accustomed themselves to. They avoid looking high above them, since heights apparently frighten them. Unfortunately for them, it is this high sight that develops true vision.)

When, at last, the other turkeys were only a short distance away, Brant caught sight of them. "Stay behind me and let me handle this," Brant declared bravely. "And don't anyone stray off toward those other turkeys."

Brant began to walk slowly toward the other flock, pecking at the ground as he went, *pretending* that he had not noticed them. The other turkeys panicked as soon as they saw Brant. Trying to regain their composure as quickly as they could, they attempted to strut past Brant. But Brant, totally unruffled, was already strutting proudly past them. Soon Rad and all of the older turkeys were doing the same. Selin followed, doing the best she could at this game. Hagen just watched.

It seemed to Hagen that some sort of contest was being played out in front of him. And, whatever the contest, his flock had won, for they had been prepared ahead of time. The other flock managed to hold their heads high as long as they walked past, but Hagen's keen eyes observed that they dropped their heads in despair once they were out of turkey sight.

Hagen continued to stand there after all the turkeys had passed. A deep sadness filled his whole being as he considered what it was that had been played out in front of him. The whole scene seemed repulsive to him; his very nature rebelled at such goings on.

It was at this moment Hagen responded to a deep instinct stirring within his inmost being. Contrary to all the instructions he had received and all the vows he had made, Hagen lifted his eyes toward the skies. Between the trees above him, he could clearly see a patch of blue. For one small moment, he found himself wishing he were back in his aerie high above the trees. Then an ancient, far-off memory crept in. He remembered his Mama and Papa. It seemed that his Papa was so strong, with large, powerful wings that lifted him to the heavens and graced the sky with grandeur. He recalled that Papa would fly into the sky and bring back meat. Once more, Hagen wondered why he had to eat those infernal acorns. Hagen was startled to see that he had stretched his wings out. Though he was still a young eagle, his wingspan exceeded that of any of the turkeys. For a long time he stared at them. They reminded him of his Papa's wings, only he had never used his own wings. He wondered why he had such mighty wings, and then concluded it must have had something to do with being born a poor, good-for-nothing, rotten, stinking ol' buzzard.

The sound of rustling leaves stirred Hagen from his thoughts.

"Are you all right, little fella?" Brant gobbled out.

Hagen turned toward him. Brant was moving his enormous body toward Hagen. "Yes. I was just remembering my Papa and Mama. Tell me, Brant. Who were those turkeys?" inquired Hagen. "And why did we not speak to them? They were our brothers, were they not? And why the strange strutting and haughtiness?"

"They are Berriers," Brant replied, almost menacingly. "They claim to be direct descendants of Sacretoes. They believe that only they are true turkeys." With his tail feathers raised in a sign of disgust, Brant continued. "We are *second-rate* turkeys in their eyes."

"They really believe that you are not a real turkey?" Hagen responded in sheer disbelief.

"That's right. They believe that we must eat only berries and never eat acorns. Furthermore, we must eat berries directly from the bushes and never off the ground. Otherwise one is not a real turkey."

Before Hagen could ask anything else, Brant spoke again. "Of course, it is sheer nonsense to demand that we eat the fruit of the bush to prove that we are true turkeys." Brant raised himself to his full stature and slowly fanned out all his feathers. "All one must do is but watch us, and he will observe a true turkey. Furthermore, acorns and only acorns are the food of turkeys. Sacretoes said so!"

"But you *have* eaten berries, have you not?"

"Ah, sure . . ." Brant shuffled his long, skinny, clawed toes in the leaves. "Actually, there are certain times when I really like to taste a berry. But . . ."

"Have you ever pulled a berry directly from the bush?" Hagen hurriedly asked again.

Some of Brant's feathers stood straight up. He was obviously upset that he had become caught in this particular conversation.

"No. On those rare occasions when true turkeys eat berries, they must be eaten from the ground. It is not good for a turkey to eat berries before they ripen," Brant responded in a tone that could only be taken as a reprimand.

Hagen did not understand why the Berriers would think that Brant's flock were not real turkeys. After all, they looked identical to all other turkeys. How could eating berries from a bush determine if you were a true turkey? Or, for that matter, eating only acorns?

As Brant and Hagen retraced their steps to rejoin the rest of the flock, Hagen mulled over the entire discussion he had just had. One thing was sure, the first chance he got (when no one was looking) he was going to try some berries, on the bush and on the ground.

"Still," Hagen thought to himself, "I am very glad (and quite fortunate) to be a member of my kind of turkey!"

Long ago, it seems, turkeys had divided into many different flocks. Why, no one was really certain. Nonetheless each flock promoted its particular priorities and firmly held that they alone were true turkeys, and that they must never associate with any others.

You should know that each such flock is called a turkeydoo. No one knows exactly how many turkeydoos there are, but one thing is certain: There are more than you could ever imagine. One reason Brant had taken in the peculiar-shaped, odd-thinking Hagen and his sister, Selin, was to increase the number of *their* flock, the only true flock, bearing the proud name of Acorniacs.

And so Hagen was brought further and further into turkeydom. In fact, it would appear at this point that he was on the verge of being fully turkey-ized.

6

It was late in the evening the day after the encounter with the Berriers when Hagen had his first opportunity to talk to Selin alone. He had convinced Bruce, his tutor, that he would stay near his roost for the night and practice his voice lessons. Because Selin had become so well turkey-ized, her tutor no longer stayed with her all the time.

When they both realized that they were alone for the first time in months, Hagen raised his wings over his bigger sister and embraced her. "Selin, I am so proud of you. You are doing so well. Please tell me, Selin. What is the secret to living the turkey life?"

"Oh Hagen," Selin replied with much understanding and compassion, "you must practice. I never see you practicing. You become a turkey by acting the part of a turkey."

Now, Selin was not as enthusiastic about her own performance as a turkey as was Hagen, but she was not going to let him know that. "Maybe," she thought, "if he believes I am doing good, maybe I really am."

Selin continued, "You just have to put your mind to it, Hagen. After a while, it begins to be second nature to you. You must try hard, very hard. It takes all the strength of your will, but you can do it. Hagen, there is a secret which I have learned. It is the key to everything. It is this: It is hard to be a turkey, and it is so easy to be a buzzard. It takes all the strength of your being to live a good turkey life."

Hagen remained silent for a moment, then spoke in a whisper. "I have tried. I have tried very, very hard. Sometimes I do it. But on the other hand, I always fail. Now I have an even bigger problem: Oh Selin, what do you do if absolutely nothing inside of you really wants to be a turkey?"

Selin would not allow her personal feelings to surface on that question. She spoke immediately, "You are supposed to want to! You must get Rad to help you if you feel as though you are going to go back to the buzzards!"

Hagen was shocked."Who told you that we are buzzards? Rad told me, but I did not know that you were told, too."

"My tutor has taught me all about buzzards. Everyone knows about buzzards." Selin paused for a moment as though she were trying to choose the perfect words for her next sentence. "Hagen, can't you see? That explains why Mama and Papa left us. They are nothing but buzzards. And you and I are . . . are . . . poor, worthless, dirty, good-for-nothing ol' buzzards."

Hagen again tried to muster up gratitude to the dear turkeys for saving him and his sister. (The fact was, after all this time, he was tired of being grateful for being saved from the dirty ol' buzzards. Surely there was more to turkey life than being saved from being a buzzard.)

Selin continued, "You should work harder and harder at living the turkey life. And ask fewer questions, Hagen. Now, let me share with you another secret: The harder you work at being a turkey, the less you will be tempted to be a buzzard."

Selin was beginning to be proud of herself for remembering so many things that she had been taught, even though up until now, they had not seemed to be working well for her, either.

"So what should I spend my time doing, sister? I am such a failure at being a turkey," Hagen moaned.

"Hagen, you must understand that you are a buzzard inside. It takes a lot for a dirty, worthless, terrible ol' buzzard to live the part of a turkey. In fact, if the truth were known, only a few of us poor, wretched buzzards ever become perfectly turkey-ized. Let us be glad the turkeys have accepted us at all."

Hagen nodded his head, sighed, and shuffled off.

7

When Hagen awoke the next morning, he immediately began to work hard at his lessons. Once more, he re-dedicated his life to learning how to be a good turkey. Hagen was so determined, that he even told Bruce that he wanted to devote the entire morning to turkey lessons.

For almost an entire hour, Hagen concentrated with all his being on getting out just one perfect gobble. He felt so proud of himself when two turkey hens that were walking nearby turned toward him at his call. It was the best he had ever done. Still, it was very difficult to sound like a turkey, and he did not feel as encouraged about his success as did his tutor.

Next, Hagen tried his skill at scratching the ground. It looked simple enough, but Hagen simply could not figure out how to stand on one leg and scratch with the other. Each try sent him flopping to the ground. Nonetheless, after almost half an hour, he did manage one or two good scratches before he tumbled over.

Then came strutting. Strutting was difficult for Hagen because he was not as fat as the turkeys. He looked perfectly ridiculous, and no amount of practice was going to change that. Once or twice he tried balancing himself by spreading his wings, but this brought a sudden reprimand from his tutor. "You have to stretch and you have to strut without your wings," was his reminder.

By midday, Hagen was exasperated. And beyond that, he was depressed that he was exasperated! The morning had begun so positively for him. Now he was lower than he had ever been. He simply could not live the turkey life. "Why, oh why can I not live the turkey life?" he wondered.

Later that day, Hagen had joined the rest of the flock looking for acorns. He did so with a vengeance, for he was extremely hungry from all his work on his lessons. As the flock approached a clearing in the wood, most of the turkeys followed closely behind Brant, who was walking the perimeter of the meadow so as not to expose himself in the open.

Hagen, feeling a touch of rebelliousness from his morning's frustrations, walked straight out into the field. Immediately he noticed that beyond the meadow there rose a grassy hill where the wood began again, and beyond that rose a high and lofty snow-capped mountain. The sight of that mountain awed Hagen. Something deep within him stirred, and suppressing it was out of the question.

Suddenly something else caught his keen eyes. High above him was some kind of majestic bird flying in the sky. This sight caused him to recall that vague memory of his Papa flying. "Maybe that is Papa looking for me!" The very thought electrified him. As he watched spellbound, he saw that there was more than one. Hagen ached to spread his wings and try to fly up there and join them.

You may take an eagle out of the sky, but you cannot take the sky out of the eagle. When his creator created him, sky was placed inside him, and it could not be removed.

At just that moment, Brant bellowed out a warning. "Hagen, no, no, don't look! Those are buzzards up there!"

Hagen hesitated.

"You don't want to go back to the buzzards, do you?"

Hagen replied quickly and pitifully, "No, I do not want to be a buzzard."

47

"What shall I ever do?" Hagen thought. "I try so hard and practice the turkey life so hard, and still I revert back to my buzzard ways."

For the rest of the day, Hagen lagged behind the the rest of the flock, his drooping head just clearing the ground. Late that evening, he leaned against an old oak tree and let every feather on him droop.

"There has to be more to life than this!" he said aloud, not knowing that someone had been watching, and was now listening.

It seems that there was a very attentive owl in the tree just above Hagen. This particular owl's name was Drew, and he just happened to be the wisest of all the owls in the forest.

"Whoooo are you?" Drew asked curiously.

Hagen, tired and frustrated, answered in a most pitiful voice, "I am a poor little turkey that is so discouraged. I am just tired of life." And surely he was the very picture of despair.

Drew peered more closely at Hagen. His face saddened at the pitiful sight below him. "Turkey?" Drew mused to himself.

"What is your name?" Drew asked, more curious than ever.

"My name is Hagen. What is yours?" Hagen had still not risen to look at his new companion.

"I am Drew, the owl," he said, and then added, "You are the most curious turkey I have ever seen. Who told you that you were a turkey?"

Hagen immediately jumped up in defensive anger. "I am so a turkey. I am of the Acorniacs, from the turkeydoo of Brant. My sister and I joined them months ago. They have taught us everything about being turkeys. I am *not* a buzzard!"

"STOP! Stop!" Drew pleaded. "You can be a turkey if that is what pleases you. I only asked, '*Who* told you that you were a turkey?'"

For the first time, Hagen looked up at Drew.

"I'll say this for you," Drew continued. "You are a bird. But you don't look like a turkey *or* a buzzard to me. Hagen, do you really think that all birds must be either a turkey or a buzzard?"

"Well," Hagen said thoughtfully, "I have never heard of any other kind of bird. Have you?"

"I am not a turkey" the wise old owl replied. "Nor, I might add, do I travel with the turkeys. Furthermore, when I travel, I prefer to fly."

Drew had already decided that he would be wholly truthful with Hagen only if he felt Hagen wanted to know more very desperately. Drew knew well that Hagen was an eagle, but that Hagen would be willing to recognize that fact only if he were desperate. Otherwise Hagen would just return to the turkeys.

"You fly!?" Hagen questioned, cautiously and skeptically. He felt that he could not afford any more disappointments.

"Yes, and I see that you have large and powerful wings, too. Maybe even you could fly. Do you think that is a possibility?"

Drew was testing Hagen.

Hagen backed away from the tree. The thought of flying sounded so appealing, yet he knew that it would not meet with the approval of his turkeydoo. "No, I can't fly," Hagen replied in a voice of utter dejection. "You see, Drew, there are buzzards up there. Are you not afraid that if you fly, you will become like a good-for-nothing, low down, sorry ol' buzzard?"

"Only turkeys are afraid of such a thing. Why are you afraid?"

Before Hagen could respond or even think, Drew spoke again. "My friend, you have been taught to be afraid. You have been *taught* to live in hiding. You should not listen to such things. Do you really want to live like such a lowly creature?"

Hagen began to sob. His only thought was, "I do not want to be a turkey, but I just *cannot* be a dirty ol' buzzard."

Drew wanted to say more, but he decided to wait until Hagen was ready.

"The buzzard is not the only bird in the sky. There is another . . . and it also flies higher. You should see the eagle fly, Hagen.

"You should see an eagle fly," he said again, softly.

Drew spread his wings and leaped to a low hanging branch. Hagen looked up to catch Drew's face, but the owl was gone.

Hagen felt he would die if he did not fly after him, but he was afraid. He was not sure what he was afraid of, but whatever it was, it was keeping him from flying.

8

Hagen became even more restless than he had been before. He would have a 'good' day sometimes, but he could not shake the words of the owl. He felt as though something inside him wanted to be set free. Whatever it was, the owl had awakened it afresh and made it stronger.

He wondered if any of the turkeys knew about Drew. Maybe Drew was just a crazy ol' owl who talked nonsense.

At midday, as their turkeydoo moved through the wood searching for acorns, Hagen managed to get next to Selin to speak.

"Selin, do you know of Drew the owl?" Hagen whispered.

"Yes, Felda told me a few stories about him," Selin answered. They continued to move about as they talked.

"Well, what did she say?" Hagen's impatience surfaced.

"Why do you want to know?" Selin countered. She figured that Hagen was heading for trouble again. "Have you been speaking to him?"

"I saw him only once. I want to know what the turkeys think about him."

Selin was alarmed. "You say that as though you are no longer a turkey, yourself." Her voice became indignant.

"Selin, I do not know what I am right now. But I intend to find out. Now, please, tell me about Drew."

"Hagen, stay away from him. He lies about the turkeys. He says that we adopt and steal away the very hearts of all birds. You should not pay attention to him, Hagen."

"Listen to me, Selin. He says that the buzzard is not the only bird in the sky. There is another one that flies even higher. It is called the eagle." He paused for a moment. "I wish I were an eagle."

"That is silly, Hagen!" Selin shouted in disbelief. "Do not forget that you are a buzzard. The turkeys adopted you and made you one of them. Only buzzards fly high in the sky. They wait to prey on the weak below. That is the only reason they fly. Do not lose your perspective."

Hagen walked away from his sister dejected. He knew that he could no longer talk to her or any of the turkeys about his true feelings. He again felt utterly alone.

Several days later, before sundown, Hagen and Bruce were searching together for acorns when he spotted three other turkeys in the distance far away. They were not from his turkeydoo. He assumed that they were Berriers. It occurred to him that he should try to get away long enough to talk to them.

A little while later, Bruce motioned that he was ready to go back to the flock and rest for the night. Hagen told Bruce that he would come in later. He wanted "to spend some extra time on his strutting practice."

Hagen then went out in the direction of the turkeys to see if he could find them again. It was not long before he came upon what appeared to be an entire turkeydoo of Berriers. He watched them for quite a while without revealing his presence. They appeared to be a happy lot of turkeys. Most of them were searching actively for food among the berry bushes around them. A very fat turkey with a beard that dragged the ground was obviously the leader of the flock. His deep, loud gobble commanded the attention of all the other turkeys when he spoke. Hagen knew that they did not agree with the Acorniacs about their food. Perhaps they did not agree with them about flying either. He had to find out.

He was not sure how to make his appearance to the Berriers. He certainly did not want to startle and embarrass them. Instead he decided to begin rustling leaves from a distance so that the turkeys would hear him and find him. As he did this he watched them approach and appeared startled when they were close enough to see him.

"Oh . . . hi!" Hagen deliberately stumbled. "I have lost my way as I searched for food. Could you help me?" He felt embarrassed, yet could not think of another way to begin the conversation.

The large turkey stepped up to Hagen. He appeared much larger even than Brant, and radiated authority through his beautifully fanned-out feathers, fatherly beard and strong eyes.

"Greetings, lost one. My name is Egan. What is yours?" His voice seemed welcoming enough.

"I am Hagen." He said no more, because Egan had obviously taken control of the moment by his very presence.

"You walk and talk like a turkey, yet you are not a native turkey by appearance. Are you from a foreign turkeydoo?" Although Egan spoke in short and direct sentences, his voice showed compassion. Hagen felt more comfortable with him than he had at first thought possible.

"My sister and I were adopted and raised by the turkeydoo of the Acorniacs. They have taken care of us and taught us the ways of turkeys." Hagen felt a sudden and unexpected thrill of pride.

Some of the turkeys standing around shifted nervously. Then a rather skinny-looking turkey, by comparison to most of them, rushed forward with some berries and offered them to Hagen. "They are not what you are accustomed to eating, friend, but they have been picked up from the ground. I believe that you accept such food, do you not?"

Hagen was moved by such a thoughtful gesture. "Yes, thank you very much."

Egan spoke again. "Would you like for us to help you find your friends again, Hagen?"

"Would you do that?"

"Why, certainly, if that is what you want," Egan replied quickly.

"May I ask you a question first?" Hagen spoke between the berries which he was enjoying immensely.

"Yes, please." Egan was beginning to feel as though he had a possible convert on his hands.

Hagen, impatient to have answers to his questions, wasted no time in presenting them to Egan. "Why do you think the Acorniacs are not real turkeys?"

Egan was wise as turkeys go. He knew that this question was bound to arise if the conversation took this bend. "Friend, we do *not* insist that there are *no* true turkeys among the Acorniacs. We simply acknowledge that they will eventually kill themselves if they persist in eating only the lowly acorn of the ground. It is nothing compared to the fruit of the bush." Egan eyed Hagen pointedly. "Wouldn't you agree?"

Hagen was finishing the last of the berries that had been given to him. After eating nothing but acorns for months, the berries seemed to be food sent from heaven. What a wonderful change!

"Yes, these berries taste wonderful," Hagen agreed. "May I ask you another question?"

Egan nodded.

"Do you ever fly?" Hagen asked in hope.

Egan looked at him somewhat strangely. "Do we ever fly?" he repeated Hagen's question. "Certainly, we do."

Hagen's heart pounded in his breast. He had only just met the Berriers and already he felt as though he had found his new home. His mind raced. Perhaps he could join them without having to believe that the Acorniacs were not turkeys. He did not have to leave the known security of the turkeys that he was accustomed to.

And these turkeys flew!

He talked with Egan at length about becoming a Berrier. He wanted to join them immediately if that was permissible. Egan stated sharply that he did not want to steal any members of the Acorniac turkeydoo, but since Hagen wanted to join them so badly *he would allow him to come.*

Hagen had not yet discovered the basic truth that eagles do not feel comfortable living among turkeys. It matters not how long they live among the turkeys, they will never feel comfortable with them. If an eagle is unaware of who he is, he may move around from turkeydoo to turkeydoo for quite a long time before discovering that all turkeys are alike, even though they claim to be quite unique. However, it is this moving among the turkeys that will eventually lead the eagle to realize that he is a completely different bird altogether.

9

Hagen left his home for the second time. This time he did not even have his sister to comfort him. He left all in order to find what his inside cried out for. Something within him needed to fly. He could hardly contain himself as he waited for morning to arrive. He had barely slept at all through the night.

The sun had not yet risen over the distant hills and the other turkeys were not awake yet. Hagen felt new. He had become a part of a flock that knew what it meant to live. They enjoyed each other in their group. They ate something other than acorns! And they could fly! He felt as though he had been created to fly. He could hardly wait to follow his flock into the sky.

After a short while others began to stir, and before long the turkeydoo was organizing for their morning hunt for food. The excitement within him continued to build.

Egan began leading the group of turkeys and Hagen through the wood. Hagen patiently waited; he knew surely that Egan would soon lead them into the sky. They moved on through the wood till almost mid-morning. The turkeys seemed to come more alive as the morning grew older. They began talking back and forth and soon were laughing among themselves. A noticeable difference between this group and the Acorniacs was the fact that none of these turkeys were looking to the ground for their food. That was reassuring to Hagen: no more acorns!

What began as a walk into the wood now appeared to Hagen as a search. It became apparent that they were not going to fly this morning. They would search for their food in the same manner as the Acorniacs searched for acorns: They would look for it as they walked through the wood. It was a let-down for Hagen, but he was sure that this would only be a temporary set-back. "Surely we will fly after breakfast," Hagen thought.

They did find berries that morning, and all the turkeys feasted sumptuously. Hagen enjoyed his fresh berry breakfast more than any other meal he could remember. Afterward they rested from their long trek through the wood.

They had rested for quite some time when Egan and a younger turkey moved up to where Hagen sat. Egan said, "Hagen, my new friend, let me introduce you to Daly. He is a trusted friend of mine, and will be spending some time with you over the next few months helping you to adjust to the life of the Berrier turkeys."

Hagen listened without expression.

"Daly will be able to answer any questions you may have and will teach you proper turkey etiquette that will benefit you now as well as in the later stages of your life." Egan patted Hagen's head with the tip of his wing. "You are in good hands, Hagen."

Egan left Daly and Hagen standing together. Hagen continued to be silent.

Daly finally spoke. "Suppose we begin with some scratching lessons . . ."

"Wait a moment," Hagen answered. "I'll be back in a second." He whirled around quickly and ran after Egan.

As he caught Egan, his question came out in an impatient and demanding voice. "Egan, please tell me . . . when do we fly?"

Egan's face took on that same puzzled look that Hagen had seen the evening before when he asked about flying. "Hagen," he said slowly and methodically. "One only flies in order to escape danger." He then added sarcastically, "Are you in some sort of danger?" Some turkeys standing nearby laughed to themselves.

Hagen did not argue. He knew now that it would be of no avail. It was at this point that he realized the Berriers were really no different from the Acorniacs. They were all turkeys, and he simply did not fit in with the turkeys. He was so angry that he leapt toward the sky in a rage. His wings instinctively caught and pressed the wind down to lift his body instantly above the trees. He saw for the first time the tops of the trees. In the far distance he spotted a large clearing in the wood where one day he had seen eagles flying high in the sky. In another direction, he saw a vast mountain range reaching up into the clouds. What a sight!

Though Hagen was indeed flying for the first time, it had happened so quickly that he had not yet realized what was taking place. When he finally realized that he was actually flying, he became afraid and immediately came down. Not knowing how to properly land, his landing was more a fall. Fortunately, the only thing he hurt seriously was his pride.

There was something else inside Hagen that was hurt, though it was not a result of his crash landing. It was Hagen's trust. As he stood in a small opening in the wood he felt his heart breaking. Anger mixed with passion rose up within him. Then he screeched out in a burst of emotion, "I will never trust another bird as long as I live!" His screech could be heard for a long distance through the wood.

He slumped down next to a small pine tree, his head between his extended wings. Surely, he thought, he had been a very bad turkey. He had not tried hard enough. The reasons all his struggles and hardships were taking place must be due to his own making. Hagen's mind continued to race in many directions. "I am a failure," he said aloud to himself. "The reason I am alone is that I am an oddball. No one wants to be friends with an oddball such as I."

Hagen sat there wallowing in his own self-pity and abasement for much of the afternoon. He wondered if he should ever even move. Was there any reason to keep going on? He was obviously a no-good. The buzzards did not even want him. His Papa and Mama had left him shortly after birth.

Hagen continued to sit next to that small pine tree for two days and two nights. The morning of the third day, he awoke remembering something that Drew, the wise old owl, had said to him: "My friend, you have been taught to be afraid and live in hiding. Do you really want to live such a lowly life?"

"No," Hagen whispered to himself. "No, no, no!" he repeated with mounting intensity. He felt that he must find Drew. If anyone could help him, it seemed it would be Drew.

As Hagen dragged himself through the wood, he began to think of his sister. He missed her and wondered how she was faring. He wished that she were with him.

Hagen had no idea where to look for Drew. He could not remember where he had first seen Drew, nor did he know if Drew would be there even if he could find the place. Surely he would find him if he just kept his eyes on the trees and the sky.

As he searched for the next few days, he began to notice that there were many other creatures in the wood. Some had wings like turkeys and buzzards. Some walked on four legs. Some had long bushy tails. Some were larger than he. Many were smaller. Some stayed on the ground. Others seemed to like staying in the trees. He was amazed that he had been in the wood for months and never noticed all the creatures that shared it with him.

There was one common element that kept becoming more clear to him. Only those that had wings could escape the confines of the wood. Perhaps all those other creatures belonged in the wood. But surely an animal with wings is meant to fly! Hagen's heart began to thump wildly again. He asked aloud, "So why does a turkey prefer the wood to the sky?"

A voice above him answered, "Because he's a turkey!"

Hagen looked up. Drew was perched on a branch of an oak high above him.

Hagen breathed a sigh of relief. "Drew, I have been looking for you."

"And I, you," Drew responded. "I heard that you had left the turkeys. Splendid choice."

"Yes, I have left the turkeys, but now I do not know what to do."

"You do not know what to do because you do not know who you are," Drew replied.

"What do you mean?" Hagen asked, puzzled by Drew's response.

Drew looked down at Hagen. He looked even more pitiful than Drew had remembered. "You must eat, Hagen. Go search for food and eat. Then come back and we will talk."

"I have had some berries today," Hagen said.

"Berries? Why have you been eating berries?" Drew asked quizzically.

"They are much better than acorns," Hagen said with an embarrassed smile.

Drew could hardly believe that Hagen had been subsisting on acorns and berries. "Do you remember what your Papa fed you as a very young bird?" Drew asked, hoping to make an important point to Hagen.

Hagen thought for a moment. "All I can remember is that it was meat," he said, not yet having understood what significance that might have.

"Yes, exactly," said Drew. "You should hunt down and eat meat, Hagen."

"But I have never seen a turkey eat meat," Hagen retorted.

"And you never will. Haven't you yet understood that you are not a turkey?"

Hagen hung his head. "So you know what I am . . . do you?"

He felt ashamed and embarrassed.

"Yes, I do," Drew answered.

"And you will still talk to me and even be my friend?" Hagen could not understand why anyone would want to be a friend to a buzzard.

"Well, of course. You are the *most honored* among creatures!" Drew was emphatic. "You are to be most envied."

Hagen was shocked and confused by Drew's words. "What are you saying crazy old owl? You know that I am a buzzard. Why do you choose to tease me?" His eyes filled with tears and he began to cry. His heart was breaking at the thought of losing the trust of Drew, his last friend.

"No, no, Hagen. You do not understand. You are not a buzzard. You are not a turkey." Drew pressed his point.

"Then what am I?" Hagen asked, pitifully. . . and hopefully.

The wise old owl raised himself to his full height. Somehow, Hagen knew he was about to hear something profound, perhaps even wonderful.

And now, dear reader, before we find out what the wise old owl told Hagen, let us take a look at that test which you took at the beginning of this book. The question is, Are you a turkey? If not, have you been turkey-ized!? If so, then what are you?

PART II

10

Take a look at the thirteen answers you gave at the beginning of this book. The answers to the first nine of those questions is *false*. If you answered *true* to any of those questions, you have been *turkey-ized*. If you got all nine of them right, do not be proud. It is not proof positive that you have not been turkey-ized. Remember, it is turkeys who strut, not eagles.

How did you answer number 10, "How many sins have you committed today?" And number 11, "How many acts of righteousness have you committed today?"

The average Christian who answers these

questions writes down that his sinful acts were three times greater than his acts of righteousness.

Such an answer reveals what kind of concept he has, within himself, of how he has behaved during the last twenty-four hours.

With such thinking going on inside of him, no Christian could experience freedom in Christ. Here is a Christian who admits, at least to himself, that his sin has exceeded his righteousness by a three-to-one ratio!

Then there are questions 12 and 13. Every Christian knows that Jesus Christ is one hundred percent righteous. But when they come to question 13, "How righteous are you on a scale of one to a hundred?," very few Christians have the right answer.

By the way, the right answer is 100!

When we became Christians, we were given the righteousness of God in Christ. And that righteousness is the righteousness of Christ. So we have one hundred percent righteousness!

Most Christians do not understand this *very* basic truth. Therefore, they see themselves as 30, 40, 50, or 60 percent righteous. Their life, with this concept imbedded in them, is ever given to attaining righteousness. Such Christians are striving to become one hundred percent righteous.

The Christian life is a life in which God gives us righteousness. We move from that righteousness which He has given us, out into life. That is far different from seeking to achieve a righteousness which we think that we do not yet have, but must work hard to get. And, of course, Scripture plainly tells us that we can never achieve righteousness by works.

Now, let me just share with you some generalities before we take a careful look at each of these questions.

First, the result of being turkey-ized is that we become highly sin-conscious. In our sin-consciousness, there is a tremendous amount of fear. (And there is an aching feeling, "I've got to try harder.")

Do you remember the first thing Adam and Eve said after they had sinned? The first thing they said was, "I am afraid." Sin-consciousness, where we are constantly aware of sin — real or unreal —is a bad thing, because it results in a life of fear.

In our everyday living, it matters not what the truth is. We act according to what we think is true, whether it actually is true or not.

If we think of ourselves always in sinful terms, the result is going to be much fear.

Another sign of sin-consciousness is the feeling of unworthiness. We are *never* worthy. We *never* quite measure up.

Yet a third sign of being turkey-ized is the feeling of inadequacy. We do not have what it takes. This is followed by frustration and guilt. Often our feelings of guilt are nothing more than our own self-condemnation. The average Christian does not seem to know the difference between the conviction of the Holy Spirit and the condemnation of the devil. As a result, many Christians live their lives as turkeys.

Self-condemnation is a turkey trait.

Because of the turkey-ization of our minds, much of the Christian life today is unnatural. We find ourselves doing things that do not come naturally. And these things, by their very nature, are unfulfilling. We are dissatisfied; we are overcome by many things. And, oddly enough, we are judgmental of other people because of this ever present sin-consciousness.

These are signs of being turkey-ized.

Now, before we return to our story, let us take a look at each one of the questions you answered.

Question #1: A good description of a Christian is a sinner saved by grace.

The answer is . . . absolutely no! Nowhere in Scripture is a Christian called "a sinner saved by grace." That is not a good description of a Christian. In fact, it is an absolutely terrible description of a Christian. Do not call a Christian *a sinner saved by grace!*

Such a statement may indeed be accurate, but is it a good description? No! It is the lowest word you use to describe a believer! Yes, you were a sinner. Yes, you were saved by grace. But now you are a saint. How many of us think of ourselves as saints? The word "saint" means *Holy One.* Do you think of yourself as a holy one? We think of ourselves as sinners saved by grace. So the emphasis is still on being a sinner, not a holy one. Such a mind-set results in a believer being enveloped in feelings of unworthiness.

Question #2: You can sin and not know it.

Certainly this is what the turkeys teach, but is it a teaching of the Scriptures? I have been taught that a bad thought is a sin, that it is normal for a Christian to sin every day. So, by the end of the day, it is our assumption we have done all kinds of sinning that we know nothing about. In fact, we have also been taught that we cannot live without sin. And so, we assume that we are sinning all the time!

We are not taught about an indwelling Lord living in us. We do not live in an experiential relationship with this One Who dwells within us. He will not only convict you of sin immediately, but He knows your heart even before you do wrong! He will protect you from sin!

If you have a relationship with Christ, you cannot sin without knowing it! You do not need to go home at the end of the day and pray:

God, forgive me for all the sins I did that I did not know about; all the things I said that I should not have said; all the things I thought that I should not have thought . . .

Should I believe that the Holy Spirit lives in me, watches me sin and says absolutely nothing? If I believe that I can sin and not know it and that Christians sin every day, how can I cope with Scripture that says clearly that God will not hear my prayers when I sin? What kind of confidence can I have?

Do you realize what such a view of the Christian life does to you?

It creates a deep sense of unworthiness and guilt and frustration. The teaching that offers us the idea that Christians sin every day, and do not even know it, came from the turkeys who do sin every day! Perhaps they needed an excuse for their lifestyle! Maybe they need an excuse to shield them from embarrassment when they compare themselves to someone else's lifestyle.

Question #3: It is normal for Christians to sin every day.

If I believe that it is *normal* for a Christian to sin every day, then I will expect to sin. I will not be surprised when I do sin, because I will see sinning every day as a normal procedure for every Christian.

But this is the teaching of turkeys. This is certainly not supported by Scripture. Scripture teaches:

You are not to sin.

Flee from sin so that the grace of God may abound!

But if you do sin, here is the way to handle it.

There is no teaching in Scripture that says it is normal for a Christian to sin every day. In fact, the emphasis in the Bible is exactly the opposite.

Have you ever asked yourself the question, "How long can I live without sin?" We usually ask it as though we were asking, "How long can I hold my breath?"

Dear Christian, living your life out on this planet is not a sinful act. A Christian can live without sin as long as he chooses not to sin. Committing a sin requires a willful choice to do so. It will never happen by accident or without your consent. And it will certainly not happen without your *knowing* about it!

Question #4: A bad thought is a sin.

It would be impossible for me to describe to you how I was held in bondage by this particular teaching, a teaching that was said to be scriptural. If a bad thought is a sin, then when you are tempted, you sin. After all, no one can be tempted without a bad thought. This is another teaching of turkeyology.

Sin is an act—not a thought. As long as you hold to the notion that a bad thought is sin, you will live without knowing freedom in Christ. The enemy is able to fire bad thoughts into your head. Thoughts are the fiery darts of the wicked one! It is one thing for a thought to knock at the front door of our minds, but it is quite another thing for us to invite that thought in, and then to carry out that thought in some sort of action.

"If a man looks on a woman, to lust after her in his heart, then he has committed adultery with her in his heart." Brothers, how often has that verse pierced your being? You have been taught that for the thought to enter your mind is sin. Haven't you? Well, let us talk about the meaning of this verse for a moment. First of all, a look is a deliberate action. It is a man turning his head and deliberately gazing on a woman and playing out an act of adultery in his mind. That is a *far cry* from the thought that enters into a man as some woman passes him in the hallway at work, scantily dressed or dressed in a seductive way.

Let us use another illustration. I walk into a bank, and the thought occurs to me, "Wouldn't it be nice to have all that money? I could steal it if the teller wasn't looking." Have I committed a sin? Of course not! That thought entered my mind, and there is no question where it came from. But I have not committed the action of sinning. Bad thoughts are not sins. This is the teaching of the enemy. Turkey-talk. Bad thoughts which are *received and acted on are* sins.

Question #5: It is easier for a Christian to sin than to do righteousness.

Your state of mind determines the way you act. If a friend of yours told you that your dearest loved one just died a horrible death — and you believed him — you would be overcome by grief and sadness. But what if your friend had lied to you? Would you feel grief? As long as you did not know that you had been lied to, you would still act on the belief you held, that your loved one was killed.

In the same way a cloud of sin-consciousness hanging over a Christian, a belief that he is sinning all the time, can so alter a Christian's behavior that he can (and does) slowly become turkey-ized.

It is hard (no, impossible!) for a Christian to live what most people call "the Christian life" today, because the real Christian life is simply not what is being portrayed to believers today.

In Jesus' day, it was impossible for people to live the life projected to them by those people called Pharisees. But that "Pharisee-life," presented as the way to live, was not the life of God! And Jesus had a harder word for the Pharisees than He did for any other group of people.

It is not hard for a horse to be a horse. It is not hard for a cow to be a cow. It is not hard for a bird to be a bird. That is what they are, and what they were meant to be.

It is not hard for us to be Christians in the true sense of the word. It is very difficult to live out our lives as turkeys, however. I want you to know, you who are having such a struggle with your Christian life: You are not struggling with the Christian life, you are struggling with a distortion of the Christian life.

The Christian life is easy! Listen to Jesus' own words: "My commandments are not grievous." He went on to say, "The way of the transgressors is hard." It is hard for a Christian to sin. Your Lord said, "My commandments are easy to keep." No, it is not hard for a Christian to be a Christian. It is hard for a Christian to be a Pharisee — or a turkey.

Question #6: The closer we get to Christ, the less we are tempted.

Turkeys tell us that "we need to get closer to Jesus." Such words give an impression that there is a great deal of distance between a believer and Jesus. The reality is that He lives and dwells *within you*. How can you get any closer to Him than that?

I used to think (and I am not sure where all of this thinking came from) that the more like Jesus I got, the less I would be tempted. And I was constantly frustrated because every time I thought I had made progress in the Christian life, it seemed like the attacks were more intense than they had ever been before!

I have come to find out since then, that the more you seek to know Jesus Christ, the more the enemy tries to alter your vision and take your heart from Him. The enemy tempted Jesus, and he is going to tempt us. Temptation is one of the proofs that we are Christians! Keep this before you. You are as close to Jesus as you can be. As the years progress you may feel you understand His heart better, but you are in Him and He is in You, and that is as close as anyone can ever get.

Question #7: We get closer to Christ through acts of righteousness.

Somehow all of us have it in our thinking that on the days that we do real well (we led someone to Christ or did some good deed for someone) that God likes us better, and we are closer to Him than on the days when we lost our temper with our children or when we were irritable.

As a result of this outlook, we believe that by doing good, we get closer to Christ. This is a lie. This is a teaching of the turkeys which locks us into an up and down life, as well as keeping us from knowing the freedom which Christ gives.

To believe that you could *ever* earn God's favor is to show what a small and humanistic view of God you hold. How could Almighty God be impressed by your act of "kindness"? He knows the intent and depth of your heart toward Him whether you are having a good day or a bad one; whether you disciplined your children today in love or in anger; whether you led a lost person to Christ today or did not witness at all; whether your prayers touched heaven today or sank in your throat and you felt far, far away from Him.

Your righteousness in Christ is simply not dependent on your performance. You are complete in Jesus Christ, and it is only in Him that you are complete.

Are you bound up in sin-consciousness? Do you attempt acts of righteousness to compensate for your innate feelings of wickedness? Well, why is it you feel so wicked?

When you become a Christian, you do not have to strive to act righteously. Righteousness becomes a part of your experience.

If I were to ask you if you had done any acts of righteousness today, you should be able to immediately reply, "Yes." Such behavior is the natural way for a Christian. There is no grey area. Your life is either righteousness or sin.

Everything you do is an act of righteousness unless you choose sin.

Sin is a deliberate choice. If you allow God to set you free of sin-consciousness, it may well be the greatest thing that ever happened to you! Sin condemnation is a heavy weight on your shoulders, and you need not live under it.

Remember the owl? He told the eaglet, "You don't know what to do because you don't know *who* you are." What we Christians need to do is discover *who we are.* We live like a bunch of turkeys because we *feel* like a bunch of turkeys. You are not a turkey, dear reader! You do not belong with the turkeys, my friend! You are an eagle!

Question #8: Sainthood is attained by only a few Christians.

Modern-day teaching could almost lead you to think that there are three levels of Christianity: (1) You can be a Christian, or (2) you can be a disciple, or (3) you can be a saint if you really want to go that far.

The impression is that sainthood is something that is achieved by only a few Christians.

Dear Christian, all Christians are disciples, and all disciples are Christians, and all disciples are saints, and all Christians are saints. Scripture refers to all of us as saints. We are made saints by an act of the grace of Almighty God.

Are you beginning to see that wrong thinking can bring wrong action? Then think on this: You are a saint, a holy one.

Question #9: To be tempted is a sign of our sinfulness.

This is another teaching of turkeyology. This concept certainly cannot be. Remember, Jesus was tempted, yet without sin.

Now let us take questions 10 and 11 together. How many sins have you committed today? How many acts of righteousness have you committed today?

It is important that you understand this: Everything that a Christian does, except when he sins, is an act of righteousness.

Have you committed more acts of sin today than righteousness? I found that among the seminary students, of all people who answered these questions, the ratio was 2 to 1 in favor of sins. If I have found this is true among Christian leaders and seminary students, just how much worse is the "average" Christian feeling? And what are they being taught by their leaders, who just happen to also feel this way?

If I were to ask you to list the sins you have committed today, you could not do it. That is because you are not really aware of sinful acts that you have done. Right now, you are just assuming that you are sin-filled.

One Sunday, I asked a congregation, "Everyone who hasn't sinned today, please stand up." Not one person stood. And that was on Sunday!

If you were going to have a day with a minimum of sins in it, it should be Sunday! Right? And on this particular Sunday, it was not even noon! After the meeting was over, I turned to my wife and asked her just what sin she had committed. I was interested. After all, I am her husband.

My wife's answer was that she did not really know, but she just figured she must have sinned somewhere along the way that morning. This type of thinking does not come from God, nor from Scripture. Such a mind-set has come to us, in my opinion, from preachers and evangelists who want to get a lot of "decisions" when they give an invitation. It is time such a mind-set ended and our true relationship to Christ was exalted!

Those who receive the abundance of grace and the gift of righteousness will reign in life through Jesus Christ our Lord. How does one receive the gift of righteousness that God has given to us? Well, let us look again at Hagen, the little eaglet.

That little eaglet was miserable simply because he was not designed to skulk around in the woods, gathering acorns. He was made to soar in the skies. We as Christians are not designed to skulk in the dark and live under our circumstances. Christians were made to reign in life. Furthermore, we will never be fulfilled until we live as God has designed us to live.

Paul wrote, in his second letter to the Corinthians, that the ministry of the New Testament is a ministry of righteousness. Are you a minister? Do you minister righteousness or do you minister condemnation? But even more important, what has been ministered to you? John wrote in his gospel that the Holy Spirit has come to convict us of three things: sin, righteousness and the judgment of the devil. How often do you stand and proclaim, "Praise God! I've been convicted of righteousness!!"

The Holy Spirit does convict us of sin — especially the sin of unbelief. Consider that! But He also convicts us of righteousness. Without the Holy Spirit, we cannot comprehend righteousness. There is a time when you may need to fall on your face before God in repentance, but dear friend, you should live in the excitement and freedom of *righteousness.* You can do that when you understand that you are as righteous as Jesus Christ is righteous.

A brother once reminded me of Romans 3:23: "All have sinned and fallen short of the glory of God. There is none righteous, no, not one." Yes, it does say that. But that passage is speaking of sinners who were claiming righteousness apart from having received the righteousness of God through Jesus Christ. That brother should have kept reading. By the time he had read through chapters 6, 7, and 8, he would have been flying with the eagles!

By contrast, another brother sought the Lord concerning the answer to one of these questions: "How many sins have you committed? How many acts of righteousness?"

He had actually sat down and counted 300 sins and 10 acts of righteousness!

This brother asked God to show Him what it was God was revealing. The Lord spoke to him and said, "Joe, if you never win another soul to Christ, if you never have another quiet time with Me, if you never pray or read the Scripture again, if you never do one thing for Me as long as you live, I will love you through all eternity with My everlasting love. You are as righteous as My Son Jesus Christ, and I accept you just the way you are."

This is the foundation of the Christian life! And anything else, especially anything built on sin-consciousness, will come tumbling down. *That* foundation simply cannot stand.

When the Holy Spirit convicts you of sin, what do you do?

You admit it. And you accept forgiveness from Him.

Can you allow the Holy Spirit to convict you of righteousness?

Just as a man can resist the conviction of the Holy Spirit about sin, so can he resist the Holy Spirit's conviction of righteousness. See that God loves you for who you are IN Jesus Christ. His love for you is not based on your performance in life. Let truth set you free!

89

Without the gift of righteousness, you cannot reign in life as you were designed to do. A man cannot convict you of sin, or righteousness, or anything else. That job is solely for the Holy Spirit to do. The conviction of sin drives you to your knees in repentance. The conviction of righteousness raises you to your feet rejoicing and praising God.

Here is the record:

> He made Him who knew no sin to be sin on our behalf, that we might become the righteousness of God in Him. (II Cor. 5:21)

God said this! It is blasphemous to deny that you are the righteousness of God in Christ. And it is good for you to speak out this fact.

It is fundamental to our nature that we *act* as we think we are. If you believe you are a dirty, rotten sinner saved by grace, then you are going to act like a dirty, rotten sinner saved by grace. If you see yourself as the righteousness of God, you will begin to experience some of the freedom that belongs to the children of the King. And this righteousness you have, this righteousness which you *are*, is not like a garment which simply covers sins and hides them from view. This righteousness is the very nature of God, and it resides in His children — of whom you are *one*.

Look at what John says in his first letter:

See how great a love the Father has bestowed upon us, that we should be called children of God; and such we are. (I John 3:1-2).

Your Lord does not simply call us His children. We are His children! Your toil and sweat will not make you more of a son or daughter. You cannot ever become more of His child than you are right now. You either are His child, or you are not.

John went on to say, "Little children, let no one deceive you; the one who practices righteousness is righteous, just as He is righteous." (vs.7)

Some people say they are not sure about this. What about you? You must read verse 8 and then you must choose between the two. ". . . the one who practices sin is of the devil . . ."

Some choice!

"If you know that He is righteous, you know that everyone also who practices righteousness is born of Him." (I John 2:29) If He is righteous, and I am born of Him, I have His nature. What can I be but like Him? For I am of His nature.

You may feel offended by my claim to be as righteous as Jesus Christ. Some have claimed that this is contrary to humility. (They are obviously *striving* to be humble.)

Well, you should not strive for a brand of humility that does not acknowledge who you are in Christ. True humility will say about yourself what God says about you, no more and no less.

We do not need more humility! We need to claim what God has given us — *freedom.*

We mope around in self-defeat. We have not discovered who we are, so we crawl around in the darkness with the turkeys and wish to God that there were more to the Christian life than this.

There is more, dear Christian!

The reason you are dissatisfied is because you have been turkey-ized. And no eagle has ever been happy living as a turkey! No eagle ever will. It is against his nature! To be fulfilled as a Christian, you must, first of all, lay aside the turkeyology you have been filled with and realize that you are an eagle. To do that, you are going to have to accept His righteousness as your own.

Do you know what the problem was in the life of that Old Testament figure named Job? Self-righteousness. When God stripped Job of his self-righteousness, he was then doubly blessed. But God could not bless Job in such an amazing way until Job's righteousness was stripped away. A critical spirit is a sign of self-righteousness. The key to change is receiving what God has to give you.

But what if you do not understand all this? If you wait to receive things until you understand, you will be a pauper.

Now let us see exactly what acts of righteousness are. Here are a few: Getting up in the morning! Eating your breakfast! Brushing your teeth! Pinning on a diaper!

When a man goes to work and provides for his family and works eight hours a day, five days a week, this is an act of righteousness. This is well-pleasing to God. Acts of righteousness go far beyond reading your Bible, praying or soul-winning.

Acts of righteousness *are* the righteousness of Christ . . . lived out in a normal life. Everything you do — except when you deliberately choose to sin — everything, is an act of righteousness!

Mothers are often under such sin-condemnation. They often believe that dressed-up ladies involved in "church work" are the only women serving God. How they need to know that being home pinning on diapers and raising babies for the glory of God is among the *greatest* acts of righteousness. All of life is meant to be righteousness. If it is not, it is sin.There is no "grey" or "in-between" stuff.

What a difference it is going to make to a man who goes to work everyday, to realize that he is performing acts of righteousness, that he does not have to wait until seven o'clock tonight to go visiting or to witness to somebody in order to perform an act of righteousness. Doing a good job, giving an honest day's work for an honest day's pay, this is an act of righteousness.

What a satisfaction it is to a mother as she stays at home, not to feel guilty about not going to visitation. She realizes that she is doing an act of righteousness in taking care of her child.

All of a sudden, *all* of life begins to become sanctified.

If we ministers raised our eaglets properly and if mama and papa eagles raised their eaglets properly, then little ones would not fall among the turkeys.

Mothers, you need to know that your baby was given to you in an act of righteousness. In fact, being away from your babies in order to do "church work" may be sin for you . . . because it is not God's design.

Does all this that I am saying to you boil down to sinless perfection? No. It is simply saying that Christians do not have to live in sin. It is normal for Christians to live without sinning.

The enemy has imposed much guilt and condemnation upon the church of Jesus Christ. It is not necessary to live under that burden. Has it not bothered you that every time an evangelist visits your church, many of the same Christians come forward again and again for "re-dedication" of their lives? Maybe you are one of them. It should bother you. You need to know that *you are the righteousness of Christ*. Yes, it is true. You do need to fall under the conviction of the

Holy Spirit! You need to be convicted of *righteousness!*

Yet the sad fact remains that the condemned continue to find a purging of their souls by conjuring up a long lists of sins.

Well, the Holy Spirit is not about to sit idly by and let you rack up a long list.

Let me illustrate that.

Would you let *your* children stack up a dozen or more wrongs in the home without offering a single correction? Would you wait until you had catalogued a lengthy list of wrongs and then zap the child with all his sins at once?

Whenever you hear a voice inside accusing you, "You have sinned! You have sinned!," be careful.

Does that voice *name* the sin?

If not, you are hearing the voice of the enemy. The accuser. Try to imagine going home to an active, normal ten year old boy and saying, "You've done wrong! You've done wrong! And I'm going to get you for it!" You would be laying needless, unfair condemnation on your child. You would be giving him no hope for correction.

Learn this lesson. It can set you free and transform your life. *The Holy Spirit deals with His children directly and specifically.*

Conviction comes swiftly and clearly in the lives of Christians.

On a recent plane flight, I found myself seated by a noted Christian psychologist, Henry Brandt. As we spoke together, we began to discuss this very matter. He observed, "In a basketball game, when a player does wrong they blow the whistle on him and he pays the penalty *right* then. He doesn't have to go through the game carrying the weight of that wrong. He does *right* throughout the whole game. The whistle is blown only when he does wrong."

When the Holy Spirit does not blow the whistle on you, you are doing all right.

We are told (1 John 2:1) that we ought to get to a place where we do not sin, but just in case we do sin, we have an *advocate* with the Father. The name of this advocate is Jesus Christ.

Be careful using the Old Testament to determine your propensity for sin.

Remember, the Old Testament is off by one covenant! The people living in that era did not have the Holy Spirit living inside them. Too many Christians, it would seem, have been baptized with John's baptism rather than *into Christ Himself!*

Question #12: How righteous is Jesus Christ on a scale of one to a hundred?

Question #13: How righteous are you on a scale of one to a hundred?

Everybody knows that Jesus Christ is one hundred percent righteous. But few of us are willing to accept the fact that we are one hundred percent righteous. That I am one hundred percent righteous is a gift. *The thrust of the New Testament concerning righteousness is that righteousness is not earned. Righteousness is given. Righteousness is a gift of God.*

To experience the gift of righteousness, you must first believe that you are in *Jesus Christ* and that you are clothed in His righteousness.

Let me put it in the form of a question. Who is going to be more careful not to get dirty, the man who believes his clothes are already filthy, or the man who is dressed in a white suit and feels like a million dollars? Why, of course, the man dressed in a white suit is going to be very careful not to stain it. And if he does get a stain on his suit, he will seek to remove it immediately. On the other hand, what possible difference does it make if you get one more spot on your filthy old dungarees?

Let us imagine that you are a Christian worker and your church is currently going through a trying time. Some members are living in adultery. Folks are getting drunk at the Lord's supper. The last meeting was a real knock-down, drag-out fight that split the church into four camps. Now, tonight, you have a visiting worker who will speak to your church. What would you recommend that he speak about to your people? Would you be a little surprised if he stood up and began his message this way:

> You have been sanctified in Christ Jesus, called to be holy ones. I thank my God always on your behalf, for the grace of God which is given you by Jesus Christ . . .

Well, Paul did just that in exactly those circumstances. The ones he addressed were believers in the church in Corinth. Paul proclaimed to them who they are. He did not jump on their sins. He said to them that they already have all the grace they need.

He began by announcing to them *who they are*. Then, and only then, could he begin to deal with their problems.

Paul went on to tell those believers other phenomenal things: that they are enriched in all things by Christ in both speech and knowledge! He tells them they are not lacking in any gift. Is that the way we would minister today in a church where an elder was living in adultery, the church was splitting four ways and folks were getting drunk at the Lord's Supper?

Paul understood that the best place to begin was to tell believers *who they are* and what they are.

The church of Jesus Christ will rise to such a word — because man acts as he *thinks.*

Nearer, nearer to God you cannot be,
For in the person of His Son,
You are as near as He.
Dearer, dearer to God I cannot be,
For in the person of His Son, I am as dear as He.

Eagles do not flap much. They just catch the wind to soar. Often an eagle will sit on a rock and wait for a gust of wind to come by and then simply spread out his wings, cast himself out into space and let the wind carry him up and away.

The Holy Spirit is like the wind. Are you willing to jump off the miserable rock you are on and depend upon the Holy Wind? Human reason cannot see you through this. You are called "believer." Start believing!

Your Father and Jesus Christ have said you are righteous. Will you believe Them and, at last, take your gift of righteousness?

The Christian life is not one where you climb uphill against great odds, to someday become holy. When you became his child, God placed you in His holiness. Your challenge is to know who you are in Christ. Know Him. Behold Him.

Such a waste it is to struggle to gain what has already been won; there is a great deal of futility in trying to become what you already are.

We began with God as strangers, but He has now reconciled us to Him through the death of Jesus Christ on the cross. He now welcomes us into His presence "clean and pure, without blame or reproach."

Discover who you are in Christ Jesus. When you do, you are going to live a completely different life.

You are going to rise out of the woods of fear, and you are going to be able to soar in the heavens.

You are going to rise above the little storms of life that drive turkeys into hiding, but drive eagles into the heavens!

And the storms of life are going to drive you into the presence of God. They are not going to drive you into some corner, cringing.

We are going to become the people of God on this earth, bringing glory and honor and praise to our Heavenly Father.

Now, let us return to our story, to that wise old owl, and to our poor, misinformed Hagen!

CONCLUSION

11

"Hagen, you are an *eagle!*" said the wise old owl. "An eagle, my friend. You are a descendant of the grandest and highest of all birds. You belong high up there in the sky above all other creatures. Go now, Sir Eagle, and soar. Soar above us all."

A chill of glory and revelation ran up and down Hagen's mighty wings. Instinctively, he *knew* who he was. All he had ever needed was for someone to tell him! At that moment, he recalled that he had often dreamed of flying high in the sky, *above* the turkeys, *above* the buzzards, with some majestic species.

"Look at yourself. You are not a turkey, and you do not look like, act like, or smell like one of those buzzards. You have the noble heart of an eagle. It is the turkeys who have told you that you were a buzzard and that you have become a "wonderful" turkey. You are neither! You need not live in the wood any longer. Go Hagan! You belong in the sky!"

It is true than an eagle does not take long at all to learn to fly once he has been set free. And at that moment, our dear friend Hagen had very definitely been set free!

Hagen opened his mighty wings to their fullest, and with one tremendous sweep, he set sail into the skies. Nor was he afraid as he lifted his head and screeched a most terrible cry of strength, joy, and freedom. It was a cry of triumph like nothing else ever heard upon this earth.

Hagen circled the wood for one last view of that unnatural habitat which so long had held him. Having taken one last look, Hagen raised his head and saw in the far distance, and high above him, something grand and beautiful. Every fiber in his being called out, "Yonder is my home!" Unleashing again that terrible cry of freedom, he lifted his head, arched his wings, caught the wind, and soared toward the mountain peaks!

THE DEEPER CHRISTIAN LIFE

ARE YOU INTERESTED IN READING MORE ABOUT THE DEEPER CHRISTIAN LIFE?

If you are, let us suggest the order in which to read the following books, all of which have been written on the deep aspects of the Christian Life.

By all means, begin with *The Divine Romance.* Then we recommend *Experiencing The Depths of Jesus Christ* and *Practicing His Presence.* Follow that with *Final Steps in Christian Maturity* and *The Inward Journey.*

For a study in brokenness, read *A Tale of Three Kings,* a favorite with thousands of believers all over the world.

To discover who you are in Jesus Christ, read *Turkeys and Eagles,* a masterfully told tale containing the very heart of the gospel as it pertains to living the Christian life.

The books entitled *The Spiritual Guide, Letters of Mme. Guyon* and *Letter of Fenelon,* all help to solidify, expand and buttress the things you will have read in the previous books.

You might also desire to read Guyon's *Study of Genesis, Exodus, Job, Song of Songs* and *Revelation,* thereby gaining *her* view of what she referred to as "The Scripture, seen from *the interior way."*

ARE YOU INTERESTED IN CHURCH LIFE?

Many Christians are interested in the vessel which is to contain the deeper Christian life...that is, the experience of church life.

If you are one of these, perhaps you should read *"A Coming Revolution Called...Church Life."* In it Gene Edwards challenges the lay Christian and minister alike to set aside many of the present day practices of the church and to respond to the growing host of believers who are seeking a living, vital experience of church life. Scheduled to be released in October 1988.

We also recommend you read *Torch of the Testimony,* which recounts the awesome story of church life during the dark ages; and *Revolution* (vol. 1), which tells the story of the first twenty years of "church life" on the earth.

Our Mission, Letter to A Devastated Christian and *Preventing A Church Split* were published specifically for Christians who have gone through - or are about to go through - the trauma of a church split...a devastating experience virtually every Christian will go through at least once in his/her life. Because these three books (and *A Tale of Three Kings)* are virtually the only books written on this subject, you may wish to share these books with a friend who might need them.

Christian Books Publishing House sponsors a conference in New England each summer on the deeper Christian life. CBPH also sponsors the New England Christian Counseling Center where Christians may come to receive Christ centered counseling, and Christian workers may come to learn the skill of effective biblical counseling.

Please write for further information.

CLASSICS ON THE DEEPER CHRISTIAN LIFE:
PRACTICING HIS PRESENCE

The monumental seventeenth century classic by Brother Lawrence, now in modern English. (One of the most read and recommended Christian books of the last 300 years.)

The twentieth century missionary, Frank Laubach, while living in the Philippines, sought to put into practice Brother Lawrence's words. Included in this edition are excerpts from Frank Laubach's diary.

THE SPRITUAL GUIDE

At the time Jeanne Guyon was teaching in the royal court of Louis XIV (in France), a man named Michael Molinos was leading a spiritual revival among the clergy and laymen of Rome! He actually lived in the Vatican, his influence reaching to all Italy and beyond. The great, near great, the unknown sought him out for spiritual counsel. He was the spiritual director of many of the illuminaries of the seventeenth century. He wrote THE SPIRITUAL GUIDE to meet the need of a growing hunger for spiritual direction. The book was, for a time, banned and condemned to be burned. The author was convicted and sentenced to a dungeon after one of the most sensational trials in European history.

Here, in modern English, is that remarkable book.

BOOKS by Gene Edwards

DIVINE ROMANCE

"**How can I go about loving the Lord** personally, intimately?" No book ever written will help more in answering this question for you. Not quite allegory, not quite parable, here is the most beautiful story on the love of God you have ever read. Beginning in eternity past, you will see your Lord unfold the only purpose for which He created all things. Plunging into time and space, you behold a breathtaking saga as He pursues His purpose, to have a bride! See His love story through His eyes. Be present at the crucifixion and resurrection as viewed from the heavenly realms. You will read the most glorious and powerful rendition of the crucifixion and resurrection ever described. The story reaches its climax at the end of the ages in a heart-stopping scene of the Lord at last taking His bride unto Himself. When you have finished this book, you will know the centrality of His love for you. A book that can set a flame in your heart to pour out your love upon Him.

A TALE OF THREE KINGS

A book beloved around the world. A dramatically told tale of Saul, David and Absalom, on the subject of brokenness. A book used in the healing of the lives of many Christians who have been devastated by church splits and by injuries suffered at the hands of other Christians.

OUR MISSION

A group of Christian young men in their early twenties met together for a weekend retreat to hear Gene Edwards speak. Unknown to them, they were about to pass through a catastrophic split. These messages were delivered to prepare those young men spiritually for the inevitable disaster facing them. Edwards presents the standard of the first century believers and how those believers walked when passing through similar crises. A remarkable statement on how a Christian is to conduct himself in times of strife, division and crisis. A book every Christian, every minister, every worker will need at one time or another in his life.

THE INWARD JOURNEY

A study in transformation, taking the reader through a journey from time's end to grasp the ways of God in suffering and the cross, and to bring an understanding to why He works the way He does.

LETTERS TO A DEVASTATED CHRISTIAN

Edwards writes a series of letters to a Christian devastated by the authoritarian movement, who has found himself on the edge of bitterness.

CHURCH LIFE

Gene Edwards challenges the lay Christian and minister alike to set aside many of the present day practices of the church and to respond to the growing host of believers who are seeking a living, vital experience of church life. The author calls for the laying down of some of Christendom's most cherished traditions and practices, telling the story of the origin of these traditions and showing that none of them have their roots in first century practice. He then proposes a totally new approach to church planting and church practice, so unique it can only be classified as revolutionary. **Church Life** should not be read by the faint-hearted nor by those who are satisfied with the status quo.

Scheduled to be released October 1988.

PREVENTING A CHURCH SPLIT

This is a study in the anatomy of church splits, what causes them, their root causes, the results, and how to prevent them. A book every Christian will need someday. This book could save your spiritual life, and perhaps that of your fellowship.

CHURCH HISTORY:

These two books bring to bear a whole new perspective on church life.

REVOLUTION, THE STORY OF THE EARLY CHURCH, Vol. 1

This book tells, in a "you are there" approach, what it was like to be a Christian in the first century church, recounting the events from Pentecost to Antioch. By Gene Edwards.

THE TORCH OF THE TESTIMONY

John W. Kennedy tells the little known, almost forgotten, story of evangelical Christians during the dark ages.

BOOKS BY MADAME GUYON

EXPERIENCING THE DEPTHS OF JESUS CHRIST

Guyon's first and best known book. One of the most influential pieces of Christian literature ever penned on the deeper Christian life. Among the multitudes of people who have read this book and urged others to read it are: John Wesley, Adoniram Judson, Watchman Nee, Jesse Penn-Lewis, Zinzendorf, and the Quakers. A timeless piece of literature that has been on the "must read" list of Christians for 300 years.

FINAL STEPS IN CHRISTIAN MATURITY

This book could well be called volume two of EXPERIENCING THE DEPTHS OF JESUS CHRIST. Here is a look at the experiences a more advanced and faithful Christian might encounter in his/her walk with the Lord. Without question, next to EXPERIENCING THE DEPTHS, here is Mme. Jeanne Guyon's best book.

UNION WITH GOD

Written as a companion book to EXPERIENCING THE DEPTHS OF JESUS CHRIST, and includes 22 of her poems.

GENESIS
SONG OF SONGS

Jeanne Guyon wrote a commentary on the Bible; here are two of those books. SONG OF SONGS has been popular through the centuries and has greatly influenced several other well-known commentaries on the Song of Songs.

THE SPIRITUAL LETTERS OF MADAME GUYON

Here is spiritual counseling at its very best. There is a Christ-centeredness to Jeanne Guyon's counsel that is rarely, if ever, seen in Christian literature.

THE WAY OUT

A spiritual study of Exodus as seen from "the interior way."

THE BOOK OF JOB

Guyon looks at the life of Job from the view of the deeper Christian life.

CHRIST OUR REVELATION

A profound and spiritual look at the book of Revelation.

The following prices are for the year 1988 only; please write for our catalog for price updates and for new releases. All books are paperback unless otherwise noted.

Turkeys & Eagles (Peter Lord) .... 8.95 hb
Autobiography of Jesus Christ .... 8.95 hb
   on cassette tape (6 tape set in album) 29.95
Preventing a Church Split (Edwards) ... 8.95 hb
A Tale of Three Kings (Edwards) 5.95
The Divine Romance (Edwards)(10.95 hb) 6.95 pb
Experiencing the Depths of Jesus Christ (Guyon) 5.95
The Inward Journey (Edwards) 5.95
Letters to a Devastated Christian (Edwards) 4.95
Our Mission (Edwards) 7.95
Revolution, Vol. 1 (Edwards) 5.95
Practicing His Presence (Lawrence, Laubach) 5.95
Union with God (Guyon) 6.95
Final Steps in Christian Maturity (Guyon) .. 6.95
The Spiritual Guide (Molinos) 5.95
Torch of the Testimony (Kennedy) 6.95
Mme. Guyon's Letters 6.95
Fenelon's Letters 6.95
Guyon's Commentaries:
   Genesis 6.95
   Exodus (The Way Out) 6.95
   Song of Songs 6.95
   Job................................. 7.95
   Revelation (Christ, Our Revelation) 7.95

Christian Books Publishing House
The Seedsowers
P.O. Box 3368
Auburn, Maine 04210
207-783-4234
Visa-MasterCard accepted
These books are available through your local Christian book store.